IS **STEM** EVERYWHERE

SURROUNDED BY
CHEMICALS

THE SCIENCE OF CHEMISTRY

JOHN LESLEY

REDBACK
publishing

Redback Publishing
PO Box 357 Frenchs Forest NSW 2086
Australia

www.redbackpublishing.com
orders@redbackpublishing.com

ISBN 978-1-922322-89-0

Author: John Lesley
Editor: Marlene Vaughan
Designer: Redback Publishing

Original illustrations © Redback Publishing 2022
Originated by Redback Publishing

Printed and bound in Malaysia

Acknowledgements
Abbreviations: l—left, r—right, b—bottom, t—top, c—centre, m—middle
We would like to thank the following for permission to reproduce
photographs: (Images © shutterstock)

Every effort has been made to contact copyright holders of any material
reproduced in this book. Any omissions will be rectified in subsequent
printings if notice is given to the publisher.

A catalogue record for this
book is available from the
National Library of Australia

NATIONAL
LIBRARY
OF AUSTRALIA

CONTENTS

CHEMICALS ARE EVERYWHERE

Chemicals are all around us. We can see, smell, taste, hear and touch them all the time.

Chemicals are not just things that a chemist uses in a science laboratory. There are chemicals in the food you eat at lunch, the soap you use to wash your hands, and the fizzing bubbles you can hear when you open a can of lemonade. Chemicals can be in something solid, like a tree, or in a liquid, like a chocolate milkshake, and even in the air you are breathing right now.

Turn the pages of this book to find out about chemicals, what they are and how they interact with each other to create the Universe we live in.

Some things are made of just one type of chemical, while others are a combination of chemicals. Gold is made up of atoms that are all the same, but sugar has different types of atoms that combine together to make molecules.

Sucrose

A CHEMICAL YOU CAN SEE

The water that forms ice is a chemical in its solid form.

A CHEMICAL YOU CAN TASTE

The salt on your chips is a chemical.

A CHEMICAL YOU CAN TOUCH

A cat's soft fur is made of chemicals.

A CHEMICAL YOU CAN HEAR

The crackling noise of a campfire is a result of chemicals burning and changing in the heat.

A CHEMICAL YOU CAN SMELL

Smelly socks release chemicals into the air.

WHERE DO CHEMICALS COME FROM?

Chemicals exist naturally in the world around us, but we also combine chemicals together to make new ones that we need. Humans have been doing this for thousands of years. Some of the chemical products we have invented include plastics, medicines, concrete, glues and steel.

A person who studies chemicals is called a chemist. Chemists learn how to do experiments so that they can work out what chemicals a substance contains. They also invent new ways to combine chemicals to make the products that we need.

NATURAL CHEMICALS

People gather natural chemicals from the environment around them.

SALT
We obtain salt from seawater by evaporating the water. This leaves behind the salt crystals that we then sprinkle on our food.

WATER
Water is a chemical. We collect this as rain and store it in dams or water tanks.

BRONZE
Bronze is a metal made by combining copper and tin. This discovery led to a great advance in human society over 5,000 years ago.

CHEMICALS MADE BY PEOPLE

These sorts of chemicals do not exist naturally. People use special methods to create these products by mixing, heating, separating and distilling.

PLASTICS
The first synthetic plastic was invented in the early 1900s.

WHAT ARE CHEMICALS MADE OF?

ATOMS

Like all matter in the Universe, chemicals are made of atoms. Atoms are the tiny building blocks of matter, but even atoms have smaller parts inside them. Most atoms have a centre, or nucleus, made of protons and neutrons, with electrons whizzing around them. The number of protons, neutrons and electrons in the atoms determines what type of matter they form.

MOLECULES

Atoms can join together to produce a group called a molecule. The atoms that join to each other can be all the same or of different types.

OXYGEN MOLECULES

We need to breathe in oxygen from the air to survive. Oxygen atoms like to gather together in pairs, forming molecules of the same type of atoms.

O_2
OXYGEN

ELEMENTS

An element is a substance made up of only one type of atom. Elements cannot be broken down into any other chemicals.

HELIUM
The helium used in party balloons is an element. All the atoms in this gas are the same.

DIAMONDS
When the element carbon is placed under extreme heat and pressure, deep within the Earth, it turns into diamonds.

WATER MOLECULES

When atoms of oxygen and hydrogen join together they create a molecule of water.

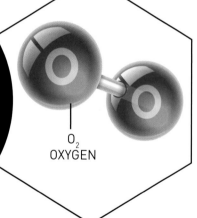
H_2O
WATER

 =

PLANTS MAKE SUGAR

Plants use photosynthesis to combine carbon dioxide, water and solar energy to produce sugar, which is a compound.

SUNLIGHT (SOLAR ENERGY) ABSORBED

CARBON DIOXIDE ABSORBED

OXYGEN RELEASED

SUGAR STORED

WATER

COMPOUNDS

Two or more substances can combine to produce chemical compounds. The compound formed is usually very different from any of its ingredients. Compounds can be broken down into their elements or molecules using chemical techniques. These techniques are needed because the atoms and molecules in the compound join together using chemical bonds.

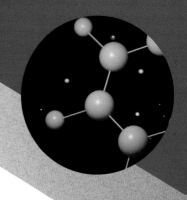

MIXTURES

When two or more substances are placed together, and they do not form chemical bonds between them, the resulting substance is called a mixture. The ingredients in a mixture can usually be separated using physical means, such as filtering.

WATER AND OIL

A mixture of water and oil does not change either of its ingredients. The oil floats to the surface and can be removed.

SOLIDS LIQUIDS GASES

On Earth, most matter exists in one of three states. The states of matter are solid, liquid and gas. There is a fourth state of matter called plasma, which is like an electrically charged gas, but plasma is rare on Earth.

The temperature and pressure surrounding a chemical substance determine what its state of matter is.

WATER

In very cold places, such as the North Pole or South Pole or in the freezer at home, water is in its solid state, which is ice. As the temperature increases, ice turns into water's liquid state. Heat water even more and it turns into its gaseous state, which is water vapour or steam.

METAL GASES

Heat a metal to a high enough temperature and it will turn into a liquid and then into a gas. Metals as gases are rare on Earth. Mercury is the only metal on Earth that is a liquid. It can be heated so that it turns into a very poisonous gas. In the past, this gas was used to treat infections in humans.

GASES

In a gas, the atoms or molecules move around freely. In this state of matter, the atoms have the highest amount of energy. This energy causes a gas to keep on expanding until it fills its container. In space, the gas particles will keep on moving away from each other until the gravity of a planet or other object causes them to be pulled in a particular direction.

SOLIDS

In a solid substance, the atoms or molecules are close to each other and held together with chemical bonds. This is why solids have a definite shape.

LIQUIDS

In a liquid substance, the atoms or molecules are free to move around, but they still come into contact with each other. Liquids have no definite shape and will take the shape of their container if they are on a planet that has gravity. Out in space, astronauts have to be careful about releasing liquids into the air in their spacecraft, because the droplets will float around.

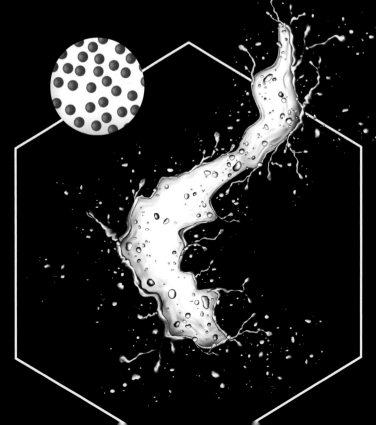

CHEMICALS CAN CHANGE

There are many ways a chemical can change into a substance that looks, feels, tastes or smells different from what it was before.

COMBINING
Just placing two substances together can make them both turn into something different.

Salt added to water breaks down so that we can no longer see any separate salt crystals.

BURNING
Burning needs oxygen to happen. After being burned, a substance is no longer the way it was before.

As a piece of paper burns, it turns into soot (which is mostly carbon), water and carbon dioxide.

RADIOACTIVE DECAY
Some elements undergo radioactive decay. This causes their atoms to turn into a new element.

Uranium is mined and used for weapons and in nuclear reactors to produce electricity. Uranium can decay and turn into completely different elements.

HEATING
Heating can make some chemicals change their state of matter.

When a hard, cold piece of iron is heated, it melts to form a thick, hot liquid.

CHEMICAL CHANGES WE SEE EVERY DAY

CRISPY BACON
A soft piece of raw bacon becomes crispy when cooked. Applying heat changes the chemistry of the fat and meat.

CUPCAKES
Chemical changes occur that result in a liquid cake mixture turning into solid cupcakes.

PETROL
Petrol in a car undergoes a chemical change when it is ignited by the spark plugs and turns into energy, water, carbon dioxide and other products.

RUST
The reddish coating that forms on iron tools, pots and nails is the result of a chemical change. The iron combines with oxygen in the air to produce the rusty coating, which looks completely different from the metal that was there before.

DISSOLVING CHEMICALS

The fact that some chemicals will dissolve in water and other liquids has been an important factor in the development of life on Earth. Living things need their nutrient chemicals dissolved in water so that they can absorb them. The oxygen in the air we breathe gets dissolved into our blood after we breathe it into our lungs.

DIFFUSION

The molecules in water move around constantly. If we place a couple of drops of food colouring into a glass of water, they do not completely mix in immediately. If we let the glass stand for a while, the colouring will eventually spread evenly throughout it and there will no longer be separate blobs of colour. This is a result of diffusion, which is a process in a liquid caused by the tiny molecules being always on the move.

SOLUTIONS AND SOLUTES

As chemicals dissolve they form a solution. The solution is a new substance that is no longer the same as the original liquid, which is now called the solvent. The chemical that was dissolved, which is now called the solute, has also changed by becoming a part of the solution.

WATER

Water is one of the best solvents known.

Water makes a good cleaner because it is able to dissolve so many other chemicals.

At the surface of the oceans, rivers and lakes, gases from the air dissolve into the water.

OTHER SOLVENTS

WHITE SPIRITS

Water will not dissolve everything. It cannot dissolve oil so we need a different solvent for this purpose. Paint brushes that have been used with oil-based paints can be cleaned in a liquid called white spirits.

ACETONE

Nail polish dissolves in acetone, which is the chemical name for nail polish remover. In this case, the nail polish becomes the solute and the acetone is the solvent.

VINEGAR

Vinegar is an acid. Because of this it is able to slowly dissolve eggshells and bones. The chemical reaction breaks down the calcium carbonate in the eggshells and bones, and results in a solution which is no longer just vinegar.

TAKING CHEMICALS APART

Many of the substances we need in our daily lives are not available from the environment as separate chemicals. They are often bound together with other chemicals in compounds, or hidden in mixtures.

Chemists use separation methods that break the bonds in compounds, or sort the parts of a mixture into the substances we want or wish to discard.

DISTILLATION

When the chemicals in a liquid mixture turn into gases at different temperatures, distillation can be used to separate them. The gas produced by heating the mixture is carried away through a tube and then cooled to produce the pure liquid required. Alcohol is distilled in this way from fermented plant material.

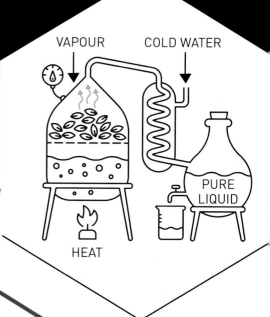

VAPOUR   COLD WATER

PURE LIQUID

HEAT

CENTRIFUGING

A liquid containing a mixture of substances can be separated in a centrifuge. A centrifuge spins the liquid around very quickly. The white and red blood cells in a sample of blood can be separated in a centrifuge.

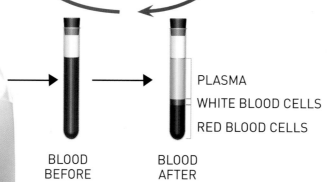

PLASMA

WHITE BLOOD CELLS

RED BLOOD CELLS

BLOOD BEFORE CENTRIFUGE

BLOOD AFTER CENTRIFUGE

FILTERING

A mixture of sand and water can be separated by passing it through a filter.

CHROMATOGRAPHY

A liquid mixture that contains microscopic particles can be separated using chromatography. When the mixture is placed on absorbent paper, the various particles move outward with the liquid at different speeds, allowing them to be separated on the paper.

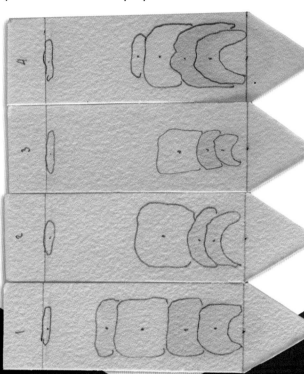

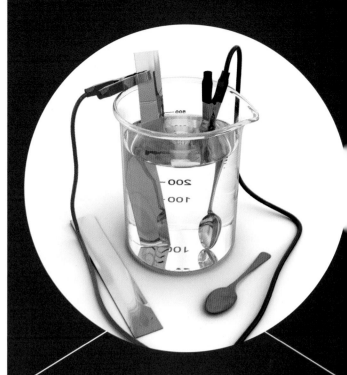

ELECTROLYSIS

When an electric current is passed through a liquid, the two electrodes will attract either positive or negative particles and draw them out of the liquid. Some metals are separated this way. It is also the method used to coat cutlery with a layer of silver.

EVAPORATION

Salt separates out from water when the liquid evaporates.

WHERE DO CRYSTALS COME FROM?

Crystals have a very rigid structure, which is what makes them hard and strong. In fact, diamond is the hardest substance that exists on Earth.

Crystals are a solid form of matter. They may be formed from atoms that are all the same, like the carbon atoms in a diamond, or they may be formed from compounds, like the salt we use in food. Salt is a compound of two elements, sodium and chlorine.

All the crystals of one substance have the same shape, called the crystal lattice. Different substances all have their own crystal lattice shape.

AMETHYST QUARTZ

RHODOCHROSITE

TANZANITE

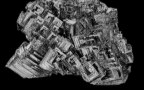

BISMUTH

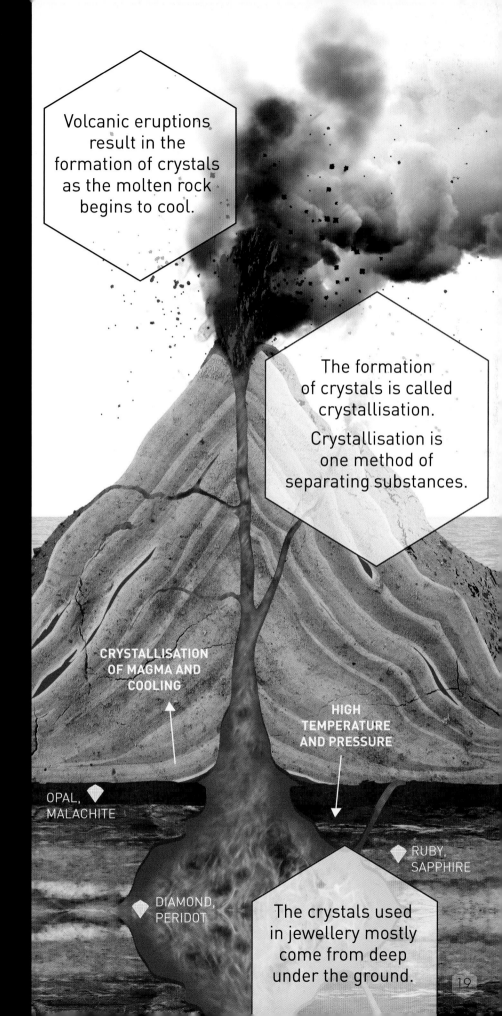

Volcanic eruptions result in the formation of crystals as the molten rock begins to cool.

The formation of crystals is called crystallisation.

Crystallisation is one method of separating substances.

CRYSTALLISATION OF MAGMA AND COOLING

HIGH TEMPERATURE AND PRESSURE

OPAL, MALACHITE

RUBY, SAPPHIRE

DIAMOND, PERIDOT

The crystals used in jewellery mostly come from deep under the ground.

WATER IS NOT JUST WATER!

ACIDS AND ALKALIS

When chemicals that are acids or alkalis are added to water they produce microscopic ions. These tiny particles determine whether the solution produced is acidic or alkaline. Alkaline solutions are full of negatively charged ions, while acidic solutions have positively charged ions in them.

ACIDS

Acids in water can be mild or very strong and dangerous.

Common acidic liquids that we might encounter every day:

Hydrochloric acid is in our stomachs. This is the burning acid that irritates our throat after vomiting.

Acetic acid is in the vinegar we use in cooking.

Very strong hydrochloric acid is used by plumbers to clean drains.

Citric acid is in lemons and oranges.

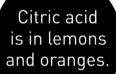

Ammonia used in floor cleaners

Chlorine used in swimming pools

Some medicines for indigestion

Milk

Soapy water

ALKALIS

Alkaline substances are also called bases. An alkali added to water creates a basic solution.

Common alkaline substances that we might encounter every day

HOW CAN WE TELL IF WATER IS ACIDIC OR ALKALINE?

Some chemicals change colour when exposed to acidic or alkaline solutions. These chemicals are called indicators.

PH SCALE

Acidity is measured on the pH scale. This ranges from 0, which is very acidic, to 14, which is very alkaline. A neutral solution will be at 7 on the pH scale.

A solution that is neither acidic nor alkaline is called neutral. Pure water that has nothing added to it is neutral.

Litmus paper has a colour-changing chemical in it. When pieces of litmus paper are placed in acids they turn red. In alkaline solutions they turn blue.

Another way of measuring acidity is by using a substance called a universal indicator. This has a larger range of colours and provides more detailed information on how acidic or alkaline a liquid is. There are 14 colours that a universal indicator can reveal.

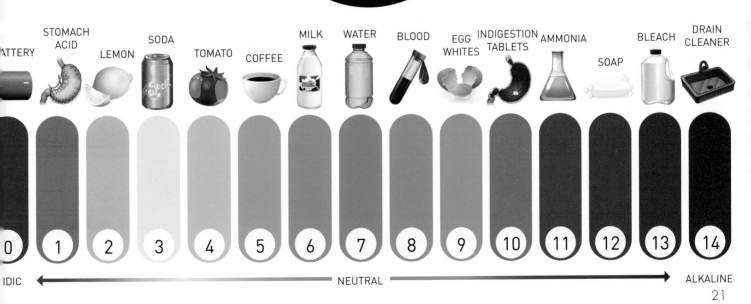

BATTERY — STOMACH ACID — LEMON — SODA — TOMATO — COFFEE — MILK — WATER — BLOOD — EGG WHITES — INDIGESTION TABLETS — AMMONIA — SOAP — BLEACH — DRAIN CLEANER

0 1 2 3 4 5 6 7 8 9 10 11 12 13 14

ACIDIC   NEUTRAL   ALKALINE

CHEMICALS IN THE AIR

THE CYCLE OF CARBON DIOXIDE AND OXYGEN

Animals breathe in oxygen and release carbon dioxide into the air. Plants use the carbon dioxide and then release oxygen.

The main gases we breathe in are:

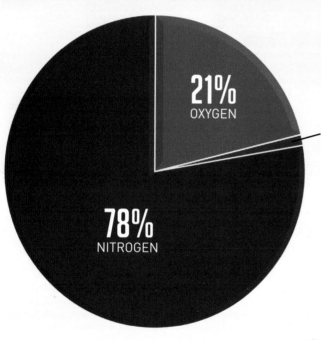

21% OXYGEN

1% CARBON DIOXIDE AND OTHER GASES

78% NITROGEN

O₂

N

THE CYCLE OF NITROGEN

Plants take nitrogen out of the soil and use it to grow. Animals eat the plants and they also use the nitrogen to make their own bodies. When plants and animals die, they decay back into the chemicals they are made from. Nitrogen is then released back into the air and the soil.

Q: Why do mountain climbers need to take oxygen to breathe if it is already in the air around us?

A: As we go to very high altitudes, the air becomes thinner. The molecules of oxygen are more spread out, which makes breathing difficult. Some mountain climbers take their own oxygen in tanks, just like underwater divers do.

Q: Are all gases invisible?

A: The main gases in the air are invisible. This is why people once thought that air was empty. Some gases are coloured, making them easy to see. Nitrogen dioxide is a polluting gas that often hangs in a light brown haze over cities.

CO_2

N

NO_2

CHEMICALS IN FARMING

The soil that is needed to grow crops has a mixture of its own natural chemicals, plus other chemicals added by farmers to make plants grow better.

PESTICIDES

To feed the growing world population, chemists have needed to find ways to stop insect pests destroying plants before they can be harvested for people to eat. Pesticides are chemicals that kill insects and other pests that like to eat the same crops that humans want for themselves. Weed killers stop unwanted plants growing in the same place as crops. Weeds use up the water and chemicals in the soil that crops also need.

ORGANIC FARM PRODUCTS

Farmers who produce organic foods avoid using added chemicals that are not normally in the soil or in food for their animals. These farmers may still add fertilisers to the ground, or vitamins to their animals' food, but not if these chemicals are made in factories, or do not come from a completely natural source.

FERTILISERS

When a farmer grows crops on the same land year after year, the chemicals in the soil are depleted. Fertilisers are chemicals that replace the missing nutrients in soil so that plants will continue to grow well.

PROBLEMS
CAUSED BY CHEMICALS USED IN FARMING

- Chemicals used to kill insect pests may also kill bees and other beneficial insects.
- Chemical residues may remain on plants and be eaten by people.
- Farm animals that are fed chemicals may store them in their bodies. When people eat the meat, they also eat any chemicals that were left in the animal's body.
- Fertilisers can wash off farmland and into waterways. These sorts of chemicals can damage aquatic ecosystems.

CHEMICALS IN RIVERS, LAKES AND OCEANS

Rivers, lakes and oceans have water that is either freshwater, saltwater, or somewhere in between the two.

Water that becomes too warm, such as through climate change, will lose some of its oxygen to the atmosphere. This makes life difficult for creatures living in the water. They need to absorb oxygen from the water to survive.

Seawater is a solution in which salt is the solute and plain water is the solvent. There are many different types of salt in the sea, but most of it is sodium chloride, the same salt we use in food preparation.

CO_2

O_2

O_2

CO_2

O_2

CO_2

O_2

O_2

Plants that grow underwater produce oxygen and use up carbon dioxide, just as plants do on land. Both of these gases dissolve in the water around the underwater plants.

O_2

CO_2

O_2

CO_2

Q: Where does salt in the oceans come from?

A: Salt from rocks is washed down rivers and out into the ocean. This process has been going on for millions of years.

OCEAN ACIDIFICATION MAKES IT HARDER FOR CLAMS TO MAINTAIN THEIR CALCIUM CARBONATE SHELLS

Q: What effect does extra carbon dioxide in the air have on the oceans?

A: Carbon dioxide dissolves in the oceans, making them slightly less alkaline. This may affect sea life that has evolved to live in water with a very specific pH.

Q: Are oceans acidic or alkaline?

A: Oceans on Earth are slightly alkaline with a pH of about 8.

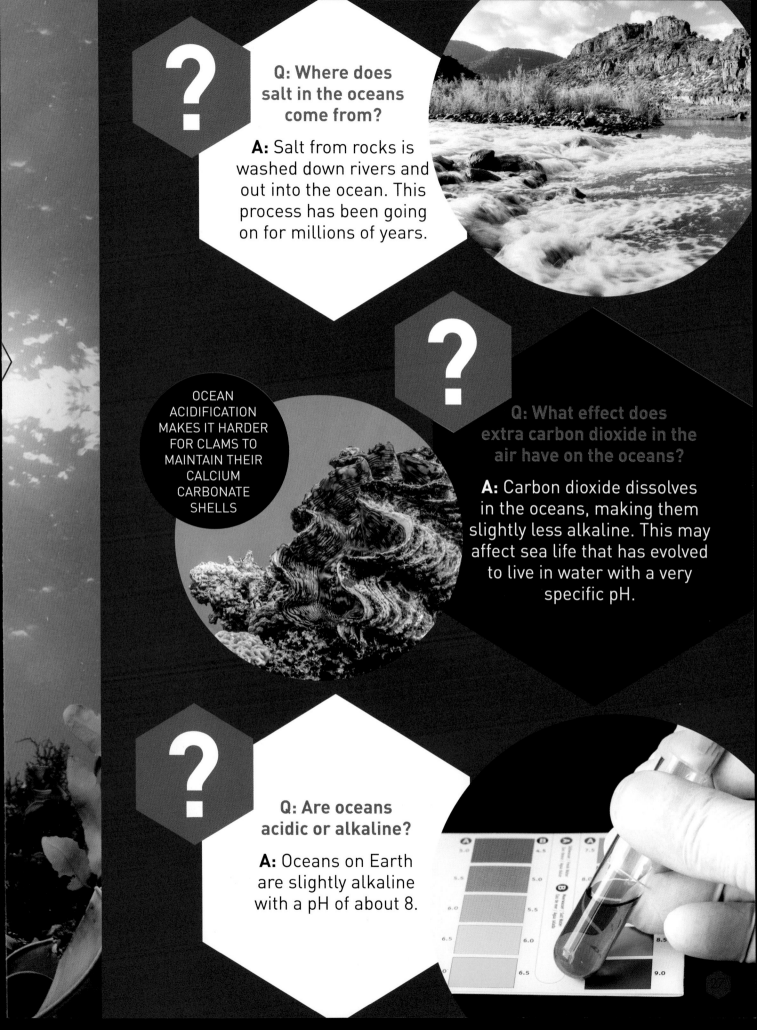

CHEMICALS FROM PETROLEUM

Humans take petroleum out of the ground and use it to make petrol, plastics, cosmetics and many other products. Petroleum is a chemical composed of atoms of carbon and hydrogen. It is called a hydrocarbon.

Petroleum is refined in a separation process called distillation. All the components in petroleum boil at different temperatures. This is what allows factories to separate petrol, kerosene, diesel fuel and other substances out of the petroleum.

Petroleum has been of great benefit to humans, but it also results in chemical products that can be poisonous or otherwise harmful to living things.

THE BLACK BITUMEN ON ROADS COMES FROM PETROLEUM.

Petroleum comes from the remains of plants and tiny animals that lived millions of years ago.

ORGANIC WASTE

PRESSURE AND THICK MUD

GAS
OIL
WATER

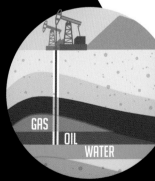

GAS
OIL
WATER

300 - 400 MILLION YEARS AGO

50 -100 MILLION YEARS AGO

PRESENT TIME

PLASTICS FROM PETROLEUM

Most of the plastics we use are made from petroleum. Plastic is a versatile and popular substance because it is waterproof, cheap, strong, long-lasting and easily shaped.

Plastic is composed of atoms of hydrogen and carbon joined together in chains called polymers. The length and twisting of the long polymer chains determine the type of plastic that is produced.

CHEMICALS, RECYCLING AND POLLUTION

Recycling of substances reduces pollution. For a chemical to be recycled, it must be separated from unwanted chemicals. This might involve any of the methods that chemists use to separate one chemical from another, including filtering, distillation, centrifuging or heating.

PAPER

Paper is made from the fibre in plants and trees. These plant fibres are made of cellulose, which is a molecule composed of the atoms of carbon, hydrogen and oxygen. Recycled paper is often not as strong as new paper, since the fibres tend to break down over time.

PLASTICS

Plastic is a problem in the environment because it does not break down quickly. Even after many years have passed, plastic in rubbish dumps can be washed into waterways and then into oceans. Plastic is long-lasting because its long hydrocarbon chains do not break apart easily. Not all plastics are easy to recycle.

Rubbish containing the metal that will be recycled can be heated to a very high temperature. The heat burns off the unwanted parts, leaving the metal behind.

METALS

Discarded metals are recycled using a number of methods. Because mining for new metals is very expensive, recycling of used metals is often a cost-effective alternative.

Electrolysis uses an electric current passing through a liquid to separate metal compounds in the liquid.

Iron and steel can be separated from other metals using an electromagnet.

CHEMISTRY GLOSSARY

atoms — tiny particles that form matter. Each element has its own type of atom.

cellulose — chemical in the cell walls of plants

compound — two or more different atoms joined together

diffusion — spreading of one substance into another

electron — negatively charged particle in an atom

element — substance made of one type of atom

evaporation — slow removal of liquid into the air

hydrocarbon — molecule containing hydrogen and carbon

ion — negatively or positively charged atom or molecule

mixture — two or more substances that can be separated by physical methods. The different substances in a mixture do not form chemical bonds with each other.

molecule — two or more atoms joined together

pH scale — scale used to measure acidity and alkalinity

proton — positively charged particle in an atom

substance — element or compound

INDEX